Moments in Time

Moments in Time

✻ *A Collection Of Poems* ✻

Mark Phillips

iUniverse, Inc.
Bloomington

Moments in Time
A Collection Of Poems

iUniverse books may be ordered through booksellers or by contacting:

iUniverse
1663 Liberty Drive
Bloomington, IN 47403
www.iuniverse.com
1-800-Authors (1-800-288-4677)

ISBN: 978-1-4759-4752-6 (sc)
ISBN: 978-1-4759-4753-3 (ebk)

Library of Congress Control Number: 2012915874

Printed in the United States of America

iUniverse rev. date: 08/27/2012

Contents

Along the Way

Things happen every day,
To good, to bad.
Things happen in every way.
It's not to be a measure;

It's just things happen.
It leaves one to ponder
Why it does so seem.
These things make one wonder.

Is it aimed at them,
Or is it just the way
That life expresses
Its course along the way?

Not to allow paranoia
To invade one's mind;
Just accept what it is,
And you shall not be blind.

For things happen
Every single day,
No explanations given;
It just happens along the way.

Changes

Where did it go wrong?
I haven't a clue.
Something has happened
Between me and you.

But now I sit here,
Writing this poem,
Hoping to convey
My feelings to you.

Many have talked,
And many have said
That you and I
Just won't pull through.

But they don't know everything,
And I fear neither do you.
That, of course, is my fault,
For not telling you.

I wish it was easy
To explain to you
The problems I'm having,
Especially with you.

❧ *Mark Phillips*

Don't get me wrong—
The problem's not you.
Those I have caused
All on my own.

I do not like failing
In anything I do,
And so far I'm failing
In everything I do.

I wish things were back
To how they once were
Between me and you,
And everything else.

Turn back the clock,
I would love to say.
Bring back the laughter
And the sunny days.

Bring a true smile
Back to my face,
To replace the one
That took its place.

Am I making it clear
What I'm trying to say?
If not, listen and hear:
I wish my father never passed away.

And that, my friend,
If you'll humor me, please,
Is exactly where
My problems began.

So now I've explained,
But what do I do?
Everything has changed
And become something new.

What do I do,
To come along to.
Change is something
I've never had to do.

I don't understand;
I wish I knew.
I've looked high and low
And still do not know

How to accept
Or what to do,
When change comes
Knocking on the door.

Confusion

My mind so wanders;
My world seems so worn.
How does one figure out
When the path is so torn?

To follow along
This twisting pathway,
To adhere to the guidelines,
Not knowing your way—

Hope among hope
For this all to explain
The action one needs
To carry along this plain.

Trust among trust
Seems so far away.
Impossible not to worry
As it taunts you every day.

Consciousness

I don't understand
The meanings in my head,
Yet every time I try something,
It always goes as planned.

Why worry about the details?
They seem so trivial.
Yet all my days are spent
Wondering if it's real.

Grasping on to consciousness,
Holding on to dreams,
Wondering if it's worth it
Or just another dream.

Consciousness—
How I wish it could be real.
What a fantasy,
When you stop and think about it.

All the crazy people
Running all about.
Again I ask myself,
Is it real or just another dream?

Consciousness—
How crazy it does seem?
So absolutely, positively,
Overwhelmingly obscene.

Doorways

A door opens.
You want to go through
To admire the view,
A mark in the wall—
As simple as that.
A mental note
Placed in a hat.
You notice the mark
And wonder in vain;
Its significance
Remains unexplained.
Reach into the hat
And pull from its space
The mental note
That needs a place.
Thoughts run rampant
On a barren plain,
Yet try to explain,
Try to keep sane;
Perseverance wins the game.
You pull at the mark,
Revealing a space
That's completely dark.
Pry open the space;
Light shines its rays
On an open place
Of better days.

Eyes

When I look into eyes,
Many things are revealed:
Thoughts of that person
Lie there unveiled.

You see if they're angry
Or terribly sad.
Sometimes baggy,
Simply needing rest.

You see many things
When looking into
The portholes
Of a human being.

Mark Phillips

Find the Time

Let's get together and
Spend a moment together,
Reconciling old troubles
And captivate our souls.

I wish I could spend a moment
Going over times
That had almost been forgotten.
If I could only find the time.

I'd build a world of dreams,
A fantasy to live by
With moments to be seen.
But time just isn't what it seems.

There's never quite enough time,
For every moment's a memory
Before it seems to have been.
But if I had the time,

I'd take the moment and use it,
Before it became
Just another moment
In the memory of time.

Forever and a Day

In a world so vast and wide,
I've found it hard to believe
That I would ever find
The one that I would need:

One to understand my every desire,
One to masquerade and inspire,
One to openly entrance my mind,
One to make my world transpire.

For all the forces in the world,
I would never once have believed it so:
That love would fall upon my door
With open arms and an open soul.

To grab my heart,
To hold my hand,
To make me see,
To make me believe.

That everything in life
Has walked me to this day.
While standing here in front of all,
I truly, finally see

The meaning of my ways,
My hoping all these days.
To see my soul mate stand before me
With such a loving gaze.

It seems my life has led me
To this special day indeed,
Where openly I can profess
My love in every way.

For you my heart does skip a beat.
For you my world does pause.
For everything feels so right,
For our worlds to ignite.

Now our hearts beat as one,
And our new life has begun.
Through our destined path of life,
We fall in step as one.

I thank you on this day
For completing me.
I thank you on this day
For accepting me in every way.

You make me whole,
You make me see,
You make me believe
In everything about you and me.

For I will love you on this day,
And forever and a day.

Forgotten Promises

It was a day
Not so long ago.
You stood beside me,
Swearing to god almighty

That you'd be by my side
Through sickness and in health
And everything else,
Promising love till we part.

That's a heavy promise
For many to keep,
Full of temptations
That make many weak.

Forgotten promises
As time goes by.
Memories of moments
Soon to die.

Gasping for Air

I look high above,
Far off in the distance.
I see a glimmer
And fall to resistance.

The pain is there,
All around beware.
Engulfing my air.
Why can't I care?

Farther I go,
Deeply below,
Drifting downward
Ever so slow.

My course not planned
But seemingly damned.
Destructive motives—
What a scam.

My thought is to land,
To let it be damned,
Stop what is happening,
Just let it be as planned.

Hope

When life has no meaning,
It stops things every day.
A questionable peril
Of a normal functioning way.

Change is in question,
Complicity even greater.
For hope is a shimmer
To be not a complainer.

Fun loving and carefree—
A longing of many,
Yet achieved by so few.
The climb is unending.

Day in and day out,
People do so strive
Just to be noticed,
Like a bee in a hive.

Inviting Moments

What do I see
When I look through my eyes?
I see a place
So serene I could die.

Peace of mind is at hand,
A place I feel all right,
A calmness of mind
That invites me tonight

To share in its way
Of expressing itself,
As I at times must be
Prepared to do myself.

As it heaves
And it groans,
My chest expands
With a relaxing moan.

All problems recede
And ideas explode;
In an instance of madness
My tale can be told.

I feel as one
With this mighty night,
To look and laugh
In utter delight.

A moment of compassion,
Yet filled with a might;
You can feel its strength
And shudder with fright.

Then it is gone,
And it's all lost.
A moment of silence,
But without any cost.

Ivory Cold

Mr. Businessman
Walking down the street,
With a bounce in his feet
And a confidence
That can't be beat.
He's got the world
By the seat.
He looks the part
And plays the role:
The tie he wears,
The hair just so—
It's all just a part
Of the image he holds.

But does he know
Any or all of
The working strife' woes,
Or of the wino
Who lost control
On liquid gold,
Sitting in the cold,
While ivory towers
Do enfold
His thoughts of those
Out in the cold.

Lo and Behold

The breeze in my hair
And the sea in my ear—
Thoughts that aren't clear
With a touch of fear.

I wonder is this real.
Can I really be here?
Scared to look away
For fear of it not being there.

But I look around,
And lo and behold,
I turn back and
The rest goes untold.

Messages Told

My time has come
To stand up tall,
To explain to some
And stop the fall.

A world was created
To help us all.
My visit delayed,
My purpose explained.

In those so chosen
To bring forth my song,
The time that's chosen
Will be known to all.

Moments Past

Doors and windows
Close every day,
Shutting out miseries
Of perilous days.

Remember not
Of the past,
For the future comes
To relinquish the task.

To better the way,
Be wary to ask,
For this is not
Just another mask.

Realizing moments
Will not last
Helps to move on
From that past.

To follow the ways
Of an unbeaten path,
Onward and upward
Like equitable math.

Morals of Mind

I'm ashamed to say
I once did play
With those we see
In an evil way.

Ever so easy
Can they lead you away,
From closely guarded morals
To their twisted kind of ways.

Not at first, it may seem,
But it soon can be
Quite evident to oneself
The meanings they achieve.

They denounce accusations;
Once more you believe
They're there just to help you,
Again you feel relieved.

For how long this time?
The question does arise.
Should one believe?
It's easy to surmise.

Assuming you choose
Not to believe this time,
Take matters in hand
And throw in a rhyme.

Catch them in action,
Reveal a simple lie.
My, how they anger
And let it fly.

Funny—it seems
You've done nothing wrong.
Ask but one question,
And you no longer belong.

So now one must think
Of all those times
You doubted your mind
And *let it go* by.

ou *have* doubted
fact:
ere *true,*
lack.

Mr. Piano Man

Mr. Piano Man,
Won't you play me a tune?
Play something cheerful
Someday soon.

Play me a tune
Of yesterday' moon.
Play me a tune
Of this morning's sunrise.

Play me a tune
Of everything new.
Play me a tune
Of everything true.

Put that old smile
Back on my face.
Dust off my soul,
And quicken my pace.

So, Mr. Piano Man,
Won't you play m
For my life b
Onto a

Problems and Doubts

Life has many problems,
And certainly doubts.
Yes, I have my problems,
And many a doubts.

For I doubt that you care
As once you may have.
That was my fault,
Because of problems and doubts.

Well, maybe someday,
Without any doubt,
Maybe my problems
Will be all figured out.

Returning to the Throne

Where's the realization?
Where's the pain?
What became of organization?
Has it become insane?

I wonder in fear
Of what may become
In just a few years,
If he decides to come

Back to reclaim,
Back to inflict pain
On those that became
A little too vain.

I know what's to happen;
I say this with shame,
For things seem to happen
And go completely unexplained.

Mark Phillips

Silence of Voices

Do you realize the silence?
A quiet remorse,
A sign of defiance
Following its course.

It looms high above,
Hovering softly
As splendid as a dove
Soaring high and lofty.

Its course not planned,
Yet somehow contrived
With a force in hand
Just waiting to arrive.

To experience its flight
Is a lesson in life:
Not to hold tight,
But to release without a fight.

To return the voices
That left one night
In an uproar of voices
And a senseless plight.

Let go of the tethers
That hold it tight,
And watch as its feathers
Carry it off in flight.

❧ *Mark Phillips*

Someone Special

You're someone special.
Oh, can't you see
The happiness
You bring to me?

Sometimes I wonder
How can this be?
Such a feeling
Is strange to me.

Some would say
It's all in my mind,
Yet time is not,
And I am not blind.

All I can think of
Is what will become
Of this special thing
In the years to come.

Will I lose it all,
Or will it grow strong?
What a painful thought.
But I hope it grows strong.

I feel secure
When you're beside,
Knowing someone
Really cares inside.

But that's my secret
That I'II keep close,
To carry me through
Till my eyes finally close.

Sorrowful Finding

There's a time for love and laughter,
And a time for only play.
Yet when those times have ended,
It becomes an open space.

And in those open spaces,
There is nothing to replace
The times of love and laughter
That show upon your face.

And it would be sin
For me to turn and say
That the love and the laughter
Continue to this day.

You know I speak the truth
When you look into my eyes,
And the dancing that was once there
Had faded and gone away.

And all I want to do is cry,
For I know I may be wrong,
Yet deep down inside myself,
I feel this is the only way

For me to find myself.
It isn't you at all;
The problem lies within me,
And I must find it by myself.

Only then can I have
Peace of mind,
To know that I am free:
Free to see and free to be me.

Street with No Name

You walk down a street,
A street with no name.
Forever it goes,
Looking all the same.

No side roads in sight,
No ways to exchange
The course of direction
You wish to change.

You look for a sign,
Or even a name.
But no sign in sight;
It's all just the same.

Phobias emerge
To cause such a strain.
Frustration mounts
Like a speeding train.

Off in the distance,
A reflection of rays.
From a sun shining brightly,
You look off in a daze.

The Actor's Connotation

An actor indulging himself
In utter delight
Of his prowess,
In complete flight.

How to convey
The message right?
To master the scene
And play it just right?

An awesome array,
An utter display,
An absolute colossal,
Some day's matinee.

Images and ideas,
Spectrums and plots,
Wheels of innovation
Centering on thoughts.

Seemingly impossible,
Completely adverse,
Yet somehow simply,
A lyrical verse.

Explain not a theory
Nor abandon in strife
The actor's connotation
On the theory of life.

The Gift

To look in your eyes
And see them shine:
Their overwhelming essence
That creates its own presence.

Knowing beyond all
The truths they hold
Means much or nothing,
As together we grow old.

To feel something more,
Knowing nothing less,
Carrying our souls
Through ours paths relentless.

Always knowing, always showing
The ways of our hearts
As they become one,
Not truly able to part.

Sights so chosen,
Lives so woven,
Our love frozen
Till death we shall part.

Knowing in my mind,
And more in my heart,
The gift you've given
Is the gift of love.

Total Cliché

To think for a moment
An unforgettable thought,
And realize that moment
Was somehow a want.

What a cliché
Of a mental way,
A thought pattern
Of disarray.

Yet the thought
Was indeed there,
Or was it not
Simply that of a want?

An unencumbered mind,
Reveling in time
Of an unforgettable thought—
Or was that a want?

Wonderments

Sand castle's in the sky,
With waves shimmering in time.
The wonderment of theory
So plain it's almost a crime.

We build them up,
Yet they crumble down;
A fragile environment
Built on the ground.

Without a sound
It can't be found:
The wonderments
That we abound.

To find a place
On the ground
That can plainly be
Completely safe and sound.

A Mother like You

For love and understanding,
You win the award.
Time is a measure
You just don't know.
You're there in a moment
To mend all my woes;
You coddle and care
Like the day I was born.
A mother like you
Knows just what to do.
When I'm feeling kind of blue,
When others have all wandered,
You're there through and through.
How do we ever
Repay a mother like you?
I guess just by being
Someone special,
Just like you.

❀ *Mark Phillips*

A Fisherman's Tale

Not so long ago
On a damp and rainy day,
A fisherman came trolling
By the place that I was mooring.

I said good day
In a friendly way.
He winked and smiled
And carried on his way.

I thought nothing more
Of the passing exchange
And continued with my fishing,
Hoping my luck would change.

But as dawn became day,
And my luck just the same,
I decided to pack up
And end this game.

But as I began,
The boat reappeared
Carrying the fisherman
And all his gear.

Again I said good day
And asked, "Any luck?"
With a wink and a smile,
He asked, "What is luck?

This game is of skill
That has to be taught,
With many ways of learning—
But luck, certainly not."

With that he turned
And started on his way;
He began to whistle
In his own special way.

I called after him
To ask his name.
Slowly he stopped
And turned my way.

With a wink and a smile
On that special day:
"My name, son, is Tom."
And carried on his way

Field Full of Pansies

Upon hills afar,
A meadow does grow.
Above dale and stream
This meadow shall flow.

Once seedless and barren,
This land was devoid
Of all living forms,
A place they called a void.

Through this girl's travels,
This place she encountered—
A meadow-less meadow,
Eye wrenching in measure—

This little girl's intrigue
Spurred by her curiosity
Of how such a barren meadow
Could live so profound.

Her challenge decided,
Her chores put in order,
Her meadow it seems
Was going to be a tall order.

For fields of pansies
Were her dreams,
Each pedal kissed
With every inch of her means.

Her life's work became
Tending her field,
To populate this meadow
Into a sea of colourful pansies.

One day fetching water
From the river nearby,
A boat was mooring
Along its rugged shore.

As Helen approached,
A man appeared.
His voice seemed to echo,
As he spoke, "Helen, come here."

His words were short,
Yet his message quite clear:
Your work here, my dear,
Has been completed this year.

Your meadow grows lushly;
Your pansies do thrive.
Allow all to cherish
Your life-long endeavor.

For all to witness,
For all to embrace,
For all to thank Helen
For making her meadow a wonderful place.

The Final Sail

There was a day not so long ago,
A fisherman came trolling my way.
He motioned me near
So I could hear clear what he needed to say.

"Today is the day to carry on my way,
To whistle and fish.
Patiently waiting for such a day,
That I may return to fulfill one last wish.

When that day comes, my fishing boat and gear
Will be ever so neatly stowed away,
Replaced by a vessel adorned with a sail,
Nothing but wind to guide my way there.

To a shoreline so near,
The destination quite clear.
As the image of my true love
Becomes that much more near.

For it's so long I've waited
To welcome aboard
My most cherished treasure
And sail Shirl on home.

As I approach shore, my hand outstretched
To welcome aboard, my girl Shirl—
My true love, my soul mate and partner in life.
We passionately embrace till are hearts can take no more.

We settle aboard this wind-driven vessel,
Turning to the winds to take us to sea,
Where our final journey is meant to be.
Over our shoulders, we see you all there.
Joyously we wave, and wish you all a good day."

Printed in the United States
By Bookmasters